STEPHEN CURRY

Making a Difference as a Basketball Champion

By Katie Kawa

People Who Make a Difference

KidHaven PUBLISHING

Published in 2024 by
KidHaven Publishing, an Imprint of Greenhaven Publishing, LLC
2544 Clinton St.
Buffalo, NY 14224

Designer: Deanna Paternostro
Editor: Katie Kawa

Photo credits: Cover photoyh/Shutterstock.com; p. 5 File:Stephen Curry going for ball.jpg/ Wikimedia Commons; p. 7 Scott Strazzante/San Francisco Chronicle/AP Images; pp. 9, 13 REUTERS/ Alamy Stock Photo; p. 11 Seshadri SUKUMAR/Alamy Stock Photo; pp. 15, 20 Tinseltown/ Shutterstock.com; p. 17 Kathy Hutchins/Shutterstock.com; p. 18 Barack Obama and Stephen Curry/Wikimedia Commons; p. 21 T.Sumaetho/Shutterstock.com.

Library of Congress Cataloging-in-Publication Data

Names: Kawa, Katie, author.
Title: Stephen Curry : making a difference as a basketball champion / Katie Kawa.
Description: Buffalo, New York : KidHaven Publishing, [2024] | Series: People who make a difference | Includes index.
Identifiers: LCCN 2023011262 | ISBN 9781534544321 (library binding) | ISBN 9781534544314 (paperback) | ISBN 9781534544338 (ebook)
Subjects: LCSH: Curry, Stephen, 1988—Juvenile literature. | Golden State Warriors (Basketball team)–History–Juvenile literature. | Guards (Basketball)–United States–Biography–Juvenile literature. | Basketball players–United States–Biography–Juvenile literature.
Classification: LCC GV884.C88 K39 2024 | DDC 796.323092 [B]–dc23/eng/20230309
LC record available at https://lccn.loc.gov/2023011262

Printed in the United States of America

CPSIA compliance information: Batch #CSKH24: For further information contact Greenhaven Publishing LLC at 1-844-317-7404.

Please visit our website, www.greenhavenpublishing.com. For a free color catalog of all our high-quality books, call toll free 1-844-317-7404 or fax 1-844-317-7405.

Find us on

CONTENTS

CHANGING THE GAME

Stephen Curry—who's often called Steph—has made a huge difference in the world of basketball. Many believe the way he plays and the success he's had have changed the sport forever! By working hard and using his unique, or special, skills, Steph became a basketball champion. His big wins on the court have **inspired** many young basketball players to never give up on their dreams.

Steph is also making a huge difference outside of basketball. He brings the same effort he shows on the court to his community, working hard to make his part of the world a better place.

In His Words

"You are enough. Your gift is special and it's just about harnessing [using] that and it'll take you places. That's not just a sports lesson. It's a life lesson."

— Interview with *Esquire* magazine from January 2023

Steph became a basketball **champion** with the Golden State Warriors. This National Basketball Association (NBA) team plays in California, which is sometimes called the Golden State.

BORN TO PLAY BASKETBALL

It seemed like Stephen Curry was born to play basketball. His dad, Dell, was an NBA player. Steph was born on March 14, 1988, in Akron, Ohio, but spent most of his childhood in Charlotte, North Carolina.

Steph grew up playing basketball, and he worked hard to become a very skilled player. However, he wasn't as big or as tall as many people thought a basketball player should be. They didn't believe he would be successful and make it to the NBA. When coaches at Davidson College showed they believed in him, Steph chose to go there after high school.

In His Words

"I first started playing **organized** basketball at 9. I was undersized, scrawny [skinny] and never, ever talked about as being the greatest at anything. And [I] had to go through those experiences [moments] of trying and failing … I think that's something that most people will hopefully be able to learn from, connect with and be inspired by."

— Interview with the Associated Press from September 2022

Steph's full name is Wardell Stephen Curry II, and his whole family is good at sports! His mom played volleyball in college, and so did his sister. Steph's brother, Seth, also followed in their dad's footsteps as an NBA player. The two brothers sometimes play against each other, as shown here!

MARCH MADNESS

Steph had a strong first season at Davidson College, but it was in 2008—during his second season—when most people noticed he was special. Davidson doesn't often have a lot of success in the National Collegiate Athletic Association (NCAA) men's basketball tournament, which is more commonly known as March Madness. However, in 2008, Steph led Davidson all the way to the Elite Eight—the final 8 teams out of the 64 teams that start the tournament.

In 2009, Steph scored more points than any other player in the NCAA. That year, he was chosen by the Golden State Warriors in the NBA **draft**.

In His Words

"Nobody could do the work for me, I had to do it myself."

— Interview with *Esquire* magazine from January 2023

The NCAA is the group that controls college sports. Its men's basketball tournament is a set of games to decide the best college team every year. It's one of the most popular sporting events in the United States. Steph's great play in the tournament earned him many fans!

BECOMING A CHAMPION

Steph wasn't the tallest player in the NBA, but he was very skilled at making three-point shots. These are taken beyond a certain line on the court, so they're worth more than other shots. During the 2012–2013 season, Steph set what was then the NBA record for the most three-pointers made in a season, with 272. In 2015, he broke his own record, and he ended that season by leading the Warriors to their first NBA championship in 40 years.

Steph broke his own three-point record again during the 2015–2016 season. He made 402 three-pointers that year!

In His Words

"The biggest message for how I changed the game is that … how I play is definitely possible … But it requires a crazy amount of work that I've been doing since I was 9 years old. So, I don't want anybody to feel like they can skip steps to get there."

— Interview with the Associated Press from September 2022

Many people say Steph helped change basketball forever by showing how important three-pointers can be to a team's success. As of 2023, he holds the records for most three-pointers in a season and a **career**.

THE MVP

Steph was named the NBA's Most Valuable Player (MVP) in 2015 and 2016. He continued to work hard to help the Warriors win, and they kept winning! They became one of the most successful and high-scoring NBA teams of their era, or time. The Warriors won another championship in 2017, and they won their second in a row—and third in four years—in 2018.

In 2022, Steph won his fourth NBA championship with the Warriors. That year, he was also named the MVP of the NBA Finals, or championship, for the first time.

In His Words

"I don't need anybody to tell me I'm great or anything like that. I have a very high sense of **self-confidence** and what I can do. But there's also the self-awareness, too: You're not doing anything great in this world alone."

— Interview with *Sports Illustrated* magazine from December 2022

Stephen Curry and LeBron James are two of the biggest stars in the NBA. They've faced each other in the NBA Finals four times as of 2023, with Steph and his team winning three times.

EAT. LEARN. PLAY.

Steph has had a lot of success playing for the Warriors. The team used to play home games in Oakland, California, before moving to San Francisco. Steph still has a lot of fans in Oakland, and he wants to give back to the Oakland community that's given a lot to him.

In 2019, Steph and his wife, Ayesha, started the Eat. Learn. Play. Foundation to help kids in Oakland. It provides kids with food, books, and opportunities to learn new sports and play in safe places. In 2021, the Eat. Learn. Play. Bus began delivering meals and books to kids in need.

In His Words

"This [Oakland] is a community that supports us … This was where we wanted to plant our flag and where we want our goals to be realized."

— Interview with *Town & Country* magazine from October 2022

Steph and Ayesha Curry believe in the importance of helping others. As of 2023, the Eat. Learn. Play. Foundation has provided more than 25 million meals and 500,000 books to families in Oakland.

THE UNDERRATED TOUR

The same year Steph and Ayesha started their foundation, Steph also set his sights on helping young basketball players. He knows what it's like to be underrated—to have the skills to succeed but not many people to believe in you. He wanted to help young basketball players dealing with the same thing, so he started the Underrated Tour.

The Underrated Tour is a set of games meant to put basketball players who aren't getting enough attention in the spotlight. There are games for both boys and girls. In 2022, a golf tour was also started to bring attention to golfers from **diverse** communities.

In His Words

"We're all unique and we all have something to offer the world."

— Interview with the Associated Press from September 2022

Steph loves working with kids. His daughter Riley (shown here) was born in 2012, his daughter Ryan was born in 2015, and his son Canon was born in 2018.

OTHER WAYS TO HELP

Another way Steph is making a difference is by speaking out about voting rights. Steph believes it's important to **protect** voting rights, and he's spoken to the U.S. Senate about this issue. He's even teamed up with Michelle Obama, who was the First Lady of the United States, to inspire more Americans to vote. He's supported causes that have been important to President Barack Obama too.

Steph also helps people in other countries. When he was in college, he started working with Nothing But Nets, which provides mosquito nets to people in Africa to fight malaria, a deadly sickness spread by mosquitoes.

In His Words

"When the ball stops bouncing, the work won't stop ... It's just getting started, right?"

— Interview with *Town & Country* magazine from October 2022

The Life of Stephen Curry

1988
Wardell Stephen Curry II is born in Akron, Ohio.

2008
Steph leads Davidson to the Elite Eight of the NCAA men's basketball tournament.

2009
Steph is drafted by the Golden State Warriors.

2015
Steph is named MVP and wins his first NBA championship.

2016
Steph is named MVP for the second year in a row and sets the record for most three-pointers made in an NBA season.

2017
The Warriors win the NBA championship.

2018
Steph helps the Warriors win another championship.

2019
Steph starts the Underrated Tour for basketball players and starts the Eat. Learn. Play. Foundation with his wife, Ayesha.

2022
Steph wins his fourth NBA championship and is named NBA Finals MVP, he starts the Underrated Tour for golfers, and he comes out with a book for kids called *I Have a Superpower*.

2023
Underrated—a movie Steph helped make about his life—comes out.

Stephen Curry's life shows what hard work and a drive to help others can do!

NOT UNDERRATED ANYMORE

Steph knows what it's like to have people count you out. He wants to inspire people by sharing his story. In 2022, he came out with a book for kids called *I Have a Superpower*. It's about working hard to do big things, even if you're small. In 2023, a **documentary** about Steph's life came out. It's called *Underrated*, and Steph hopes it can remind people how important it is to work hard and believe in yourself.

Stephen Curry isn't underrated anymore. Now, he wants to make sure every kid who feels underrated has a chance to be a champion.

In His Words

"It's amazing to know that that story can inspire people to keep on keeping on, to surround yourself with amazing people, to push through the doubts ... push through the times when people kind of count you out."

— Answer after a viewing of *Underrated* in January 2023

Be Like Stephen Curry!

Donate, or give, books to your community or school library.

Support your family members and friends when they're doing something that's important to them.

Believe in yourself, and work hard to reach your goals.

Raise money for groups that help kids in your community.

Remind the adults in your life to vote.

Collect food to donate to groups that feed the hungry in your community.

If you play sports, be a good teammate.

Volunteer in your community.

Stephen Curry has shown his fans that you can make a difference no matter how big or small you are by using your unique skills. This is true on the basketball court, but it's also true in your community!

GLOSSARY

career: A period of time spent doing a job or activity.

champion: A winner of a championship—a contest to find out who is the best player or team in a sport.

diverse: Including many different kinds of people.

documentary: A nonfiction movie or television program presenting facts about someone or something.

draft: An event where sports teams choose players to play for them.

inspire: To move someone to do something great.

organized: Put together in a formal way with leaders and rules for doing things.

protect: To keep safe.

self-confidence: The belief that you can do something well.

volunteer: To do something to help because you want to do it.

FOR MORE INFORMATION

WEBSITES

NBA: Stephen Curry

www.nba.com/player/201939/stephen-curry

Visit Stephen Curry's page on the NBA website to find facts, news stories, and videos about him.

SC30 Inc.

sc30.com/

Stephen Curry's official website has links to learn more about his basketball career, his foundation, the Underrated Tour, and much more.

BOOKS

Levit, Joseph. *Meet Stephen Curry*. Minneapolis, MN: Lerner Publications, 2023.

Lilley, Matt. *Stephen Curry*. North Mankato, MN: Capstone Press, 2020.

Walker, Hubert. *Stephen Curry: Basketball Star*. Lake Elmo, MN: Focus Readers, 2021.

INDEX